# Awareness Beyond Mind

## Verses in Haiku and Senryu Style

Kenneth Verity

# E L E M E N T

Shaftesbury, Dorset ● Rockport, Massachusetts
Brisbane, Queensland

Text © Kenneth Verity 1996

First published in Great Britain in 1996 by
Element Books Limited
Shaftesbury, Dorset SP7 8BP

Published in the USA in 1996 by
Element Books, Inc.
PO Box 830, Rockport, MA 01966

Published in Australia in 1996 by
Element Books Limited
for Jacaranda Wiley Limited
33 Park Road, Milton, Brisbane 4064

Cover illustration (*A falconer*, Japan, Meiji period) by courtesy of
The British Museum
Cover design by Max Fairbrother
Page design by Roger Lightfoot
Typeset by WestKey Limited, Falmouth, Cornwall
Printed & bound In Great Britain by
Hartnolls Limited, Bodmin, Cornwall.

British Library Cataloguing in Publication
data available

Library of Congress Cataloging in Publication
data available

ISBN 1–85230–819–2

# Contents

# *Illustrations*

*Dedicated to Yoshikazu Iwamoto*

## Acknowledgements

I am indebted to Arthur Farndell and John Mercer for their careful reading of the manuscript and their helpful suggestions. I am grateful to the Trustees of the British Museum and the Victoria and Albert Museum for their kind permission to reproduce some of the illustrations used in this book.

# Foreword

For many readers in the West, the substance of haiku and senryu verse-forms can seem as remote as their country of origin. The works of great Japanese poets have reached us through the mist of translation, from an era of which we know little and with images whose cultural significance we find difficult to grasp. Furthermore, the verses are informed by a philosophical and spiritual tradition seldom encountered in our literature and little understood, except by those for whom it has been a subject of dedicated study.

In one sense haiku and senryu have a single subject matter – realization of the moment 'now'; in another sense, the true subject of the verse is the reader. As we read, we are taken to the writer's moment of experience without needing explanation or rationalization to share the insight of that moment. The mark of a fine writer of haiku and senryu is the precision with which the experience is conveyed to the reader and the awakening that results.

In this second book of haiku and senryu by Kenneth Verity, we are invited to share such moments in a way that allows the Western reader a fuller comprehension and connection with the text and hence with the mind of the writer. The verses, written in English and using images within our experience, are from a poet whose mastery of the form is matched by his profound understanding of the spiritual teaching which shines through them.

In his first volume of haiku, *Breathing with the Mind* (Element, 1993), Kenneth Verity offered us a scholarly history and description of the form of the verse as well as guidelines for the aspiring writer. This complementary volume offers the reader an account of the spiritual background to the poetry, in an essay which could stand alone as a concise introduction to relevant Eastern philosophy. In the text, the author draws to our attention the importance of such concepts as 'now', 'emptiness' and 'no-mind', as well as a description of significant practices in eastern monasteries, such as kōan study and meditation. He reveals the historical and philosophical links between Hinduism, Buddhism, Confucianism and Zen, showing how these great teachings came to inform and sustain the minds of writers of haiku and senryu. The essence of this same teaching constitutes the quiet centre of the verse in this volume.

John Mercer

# Chronological Tables

| INDIA | |
|---|---|
| Indus Valley Civilization, (Harappā and Mohenjo Daro) | c3000–1500 BC |
| Āryan invasion | 1500 BC |
| Composition of Rig Veda | 1500–900 BC |
| Upanishads; caste system established | 1500–500 BC |
| Āryans in Indus River basin | 1000 BC |
| Vedic religion established | 800 BC |
| Development of Jainism | 6th century BC |
| Gautama Buddha | 563–483 BC |
| Darius invades Punjab | 514–512 BC |
| Alexander the Great in India | 327–325 BC |
| Emperor Ashoka unifies most of India and actively promulgates Buddhist principles | 274–237 BC |

## CHINA

**BRONZE AGE (c1700 BC–AD 220)**

| | |
|---|---|
| Zhou dynasty | 1027–221 BC |
| Qin dynasty | 221–207 BC |
| Han dynasty | 206 BC–AD 220 |
| | |
| Six Dynasties Period | AD 220–580 |
| Sui dynasty | AD 581–618 |
| Tang dynasty | AD 618–906 |
| Liao dynasty | AD 907–1125 |
| | |
| Five Dynasties Period | AD 907–960 |
| Song dynasty | AD 960–1279 |
| Jin dynasty | AD 1115–1234 |
| Yuan dynasty | AD 1280–1368 |
| Ming dynasty | AD 1368–1644 |
| Qing dynasty | AD 1644–1911 |

## KOREA

| | |
|---|---|
| Three Kingdoms Period: (Koguryo, Paekche, Silla) | 1st century BC to 7th century AD |
| Great Silla Kingdom | AD 668–918 |
| Koryo Period | AD 918–1392 |
| Yi Period | AD 1392–1910 |

## JAPAN

| | |
|---|---|
| Jōmon, Yayoi, Kofun Periods | date unknown – AD 552 |
| Asuka Period | AD 552–645 |
| Nara Period | AD 645–794 |
| Heian Period | AD 794–1185 |
| Kamakura Period | AD 1185–1333 |
| Muromachi Period | AD 1333–1573 |
| Momoyama Period | AD 1573–1614 |
| Edo Period | AD 1614–1868 |
| Modern Period | AD 1868 to date. |

# Introduction

## Synopsis

The particular character of *Haiku* poetry derives from Zen philosophy but its foundations are rooted in Buddhism, which originated in India. Eventually, Buddhism reached China, where it encountered the indigenous philosophy of Taoism, a non-intellectual simple faith. Having absorbed the acute penetration of Buddhist thought and interacted with it, the coalescent result moved to Japan. In Japan, Chinese Buddhism encountered a rugged down-to-earth spiritual rigour and from the conjunction came the synthesis which emerged as Zen with its *kōans* (pronounced kō-ans). The vigour of Zen Buddhism influenced the thriving poetry of feudal Japan and out of a series of transitions came the *haiku*. Its emergence as a statement of verse-philosophy was powered by the major surge in mankind's spiritual quest which took place in India. This is where an in-depth study of the development of haiku should begin.

# India

In the Indus Valley an indigenous civilization had flourished from about 2500 BC. This started slowly to disintegrate around 1500 BC, after invasions by Āryans, who arrived in successive waves through the mountain passes of the North-West. These early expansionist Āryans were semi-nomadic pastoral peoples, who brought with them a religion centred on scriptures called *Vedas*. The word 'Veda' is a Sanskrit word meaning 'knowledge, sacred teachings'; these are Hinduism's oldest scriptures. The word 'Hindu' (of Persian origin) was used by the 12th-century Muslim invaders of Northern India to describe the original population of Hind (India). 'Hinduism' means literally 'the belief of the people of India'.

The people of the Indus Valley civilization, where Hinduism began, had experienced no significant contact with Biblical theologies. As a religion, Hinduism is not concerned with the questions raised by Western faiths; nor does it insist on particular beliefs about God or gods. Hindus have a relaxed attitude towards theology but, like most peoples perceiving a threat to life from their environment, they sought the assistance of superhuman or divine resources to sustain life and to achieve transition to the highest state of blessedness. As has happened with many pastoral peoples, the basic needs of India's farmers heavily influenced their early religious mythology. Their gods and goddesses were closely involved with fertility and that vital necessity, water. Most rituals, even today, involve preliminary bathings, sprinklings, sippings and libations to a deity – all of them ceremonial uses of water.

The invading Āryans had no system of writing but had brought with them from Iran a tradition of oral poetry and, from such evidence as the Rig Veda hymns, they seem to have taken particular delight in their language. This oral tradition, with its systems of memorization, ensured that when the Vedas came to be written down they were already established and complete. The Sanskrit language, in which early Hindu literature is written, belongs to the Indo-European language-family and many Sanskrit words (in modified form) are found in Western languages.

Followers of the Vedic religion had compiled its scriptures and established its religious practices by 800 BC; throughout the following two centuries it developed vigorously. But by 600 BC much of the population was disillusioned and had turned to Jainism and Buddhism in direct challenge to the Brahmanic priesthood, rejecting the materialistic goals and bloody sacrifices of the Vedic rituals. An aspect of Buddhism's popularity was that it did not interpose an avaricious and powerful priestly caste between the people and their source of spiritual nourishment. Many of the priestly guilds relinquished the old rites, turning instead to mystical contemplation of *Brahman* as the omnipresent and omnipotent power. Between 600 and 500 BC, Indian society entered a period of fundamental transformation and classical Hinduism gradually evolved to provide the spiritually structured life for most Indians during the next 2,000 years.

Between the 6th and 2nd centuries BC a new literary form emerged – the *sūtra* (a 'thread'). A sūtra contains succinct but comprehensive allusion to a subject, embodying the results of study and understanding, but designed into a form which may be memorized by students. (The Japanese haiku and the sūtra have this compression of meaning in common.) Assimilated by rote learning, the sūtras gave followers access to an elaborate body of knowledge. An example is a collection of writings called the *Dharma-Sūtras* (dharma is an abstract concept meaning 'pattern of right living'). These writings were probably mainly composed between the 6th and 2nd centuries BC.

An important esoteric development occurred in Hinduism, which became known as *Jnānamarga*, or 'The Way of Knowledge'. It evolved from the seeking by Hindu sages for special knowledge which would give mastery over the innermost questions of life. It was no less than the search for a key to the reality underlying the created universe; the single essence behind all diversity which pervades relativity. This supreme absolute, *Brahman* (defined as the Divine Ground of existence) is, for Hindus, the impersonal Supreme Reality. The 'Way of Knowledge' assumed its fullest expression in certain compositions of scripture called *Upanishads*. The word '*Upanishad*' means 'to sit down near to' the feet of the *guru* (teacher) to hear the full and final tuition of sages articulating the Vedic revelation.

The ultimate realization was that our real self is a unique metaphysical reality, characterized by consciousness. According to Hindu understanding, the Ātman (the real immortal self of human beings) is the non-participating witness which is beyond body and thought. As absolute consciousness it is identical with Brahman, the Reality behind the appearance. Because the Ātman in the individual has total correspondence of identity with Universal Brahman, its unique characteristics – eternal absolute being, absolute consciousness, and absolute bliss – are identical with those of Brahman. Ātman is beyond concepts. In living beings, the Ātman is the vital principle sustaining life and unifying the embodied self. Consequently when this spirit departs a corpse is left, but there is no person. In this formulation of identical Brahman and Ātman, two fundamental questions have converged: 'What is the universe?' and 'What am I?' Implied in this is an immanent Presence which is ever existent and is one.

The Upanishads refer to the undivided and all-inclusive Brahman as *the* Reality, and the multiform world of experience as dreamlike unreality – an illusion (*māyā*). Because experience seems real enough to the senses, the question arises, how can there be two realities? Facing this intractable question with only the obscure brevity of the Brahma-Sūtras for reference, humanity needed an interpretive teacher to explain the apparent duality and offer a helpful commentary on obscure scriptures.

At this juncture just such a master-teacher appeared – Shankara or Shankarāchārya (AD 788–820). His name means 'he who brings blessings'. Shankara was a philosopher, poet, scholar, mystic and reformer. Because so many Hindus were defecting to Buddhism, Shankara coupled his zealous reforms of Hinduism with a powerful attack on Buddhism. Despite his short lifespan of 32 years, he composed numerous major works and founded a number of monasteries. The chief of these is Shringiri in South India; next in importance are Puri in the East, Dvārakā in the West and Badarinath in the North – the Himalayan region. These four seats, each occupied by a specially selected incumbent of outstanding scholarship (a *Shankarāchārya*), exist to this day. These wise teachers are available for consultation by seekers of truth, statesmen requiring advice or any well-intentioned enquirer who obtains an audience.

Shankara's great contribution to the spiritual life

of the human race was to promote *Advaita-Vedānta* (Advaita means 'not two'). Advaita-Vedānta reveals that the manifest Creation and the Ultimate Creative Principle are identical but distinct, (as the gold in a gold ring is independent of the ring). But it is important to recognize that creation is *totally dependent* upon the Creative Principle; the Creative Principle on the other hand, is independent and stands alone – it is Absolute. Modern particle-physicists have discovered that matter consists of continually moving fields of energy. Vedāntic sages had already identified the finest level of that energy as, in reality, Consciousness. Human beings perceive the physical universe as *apparent* reality because they operate with the gross senses of the ego-limited body. Totally identified with the mind-body entity, each person considers it to be 'me' or myself. With this point of view, the human mind superimposes upon the real and unchanging Consciousness an ever-changing manifest world of names and shapes, taking it to be true.

To demonstrate this misconception, Shankara produced what has become one of his best-known teaching images – the metaphor of a piece of rope, mistaken in the semi-darkness for a snake. The misconception causes stress and fear but as soon as the rope is recognized to be rope, the mind is reassured and does not convert it back into a snake. The mistaken view seems very real and the anxiety it produces is actual. Advaita explains that we, in our ignorance, continually impose the idea 'snake' (the manifest world) upon the 'rope' (Brahman). This quintessential teaching is expressed by Shankara in a single sentence: '*Brahman* alone is real, the world is appearance; the Self is nothing but *Brahman*.' The gold ring *is* gold!

The expression 'Self-realization' is often encountered in connection with Advaita Vedānta. It should be understood that, in this context, the word 'realized' does not mean 'to be made real' but rather 'to be experienced as the sole reality'. The Self to be realized is not the object of an act but the ever-existent, absolute reality. It *is* that real Self whose presence the ego obscures by seeming to be real.

While Shankara was bringing his perception and erudition to bear upon the structure and content of Hinduism, another great faith, Buddhism, was now several hundred years old. Shankara's reforms affected Buddhism and hence the development of Japanese poetry, so it is necessary to see how Buddhism began.

### Buddhism

Buddhism, which has existed for 2,500 years, traces its origin to the historical founder Siddhārtha Gautama. Born around 560 BC into a noble family of the Shākya Clan in Kapilavastu (a city in present-day

Nepal), the Buddha was carefully brought up in wealthy circumstances and married Yashodharā at 16. At 29, and after the birth of his son Rāhula, he departed from his family and studied with various ascetic teachers without, however, achieving his goal of spiritual liberation. Finally, he turned to meditation and at 35, realized complete enlightenment. (*Buddha* means 'awakened one'.)

At first the Buddha remained silent, aware of the impossibility of conveying directly what he had experienced. But gradually, at the request of others, he began to expound insights drawn from his experience of awakening. He spent the remainder of his life teaching and died at the age of 80 after, it is said, having eaten some spoiled food. Siddhārtha Gautama came to be known as *Shākyamuni* (sage of the Shākya Clan).

Buddhism is preoccupied with the universal phenomenon of suffering and its elimination by the eradication of desire. What the Buddha actually taught is a matter of some dispute but the essence of his ideas is expressed in the Four Noble Truths:

1  Life is psychologically painful.
2  The origin of the pain is desire.
3  Cessation of pain follows the ending of desire.
4  The way to achieve this is the Noble Eightfold Path (a set of rules for right living).

Buddha had discovered the Middle Way between the extremes of self-indulgence and self-mortification.

It seems that he described life as suffering in acknowledgement of the fact that people are always trying to get something from experience that it cannot provide. This unrealistic approach causes constant frustration and, because this is unpleasant, people habitually misrepresent experience so that it will at least *seem* to be pleasant. By perceiving selectively, and remembering only what feeds the ego, the human race is afflicted as with a disease. There is craving of all kinds (including seeking for union with Absolute Being) which is totally unrealistic because it cannot be satisfied. Yearning for expansion of being is perpetuated by our ignorance, which causes us to imagine that we are only the ego and therefore need to be united with that reality which, without realizing it, we already are. The ghost-like ego is often recognized to be unreal, so we seek to expand it into something unlimited, or connect it with the unity by a bridging relationship. The truth is that we are not separate from the total Unity.

According to the teachings of Buddhism, the world of our experience is constantly changing; it is a cycle of birth-life-death (*samsāra*). Because we instinctively seek permanence in experience, we find it a constant source of disappointment and suffering. If we could learn to transcend the desire to get from life what it cannot provide, suffering would cease. If we could live within the dimensions which experience can actually provide, life would no longer frustrate us.

Our experience is, however, partly illusory. The illusion consists in taking as completely real the distinctions and limitations created by the mind. In Buddhism the truth is called *Nirvāna*, (a Sanskrit word meaning 'extinction'). It is also used in the sense of 'a blowing out' as in extinguishing a candle flame. Nirvāna is sometimes called *Sameness* because it is free from all distinctions, and also called the *Void* because there is a complete absence of limiting conditions. The Buddha realized that his nature is not that of a limited personal ego but is conditionless Nirvāna. Nirvāna is therefore also called *Buddha-nature*.

The two schools of Buddhism are the *Mahāyāna* and *Hinayāna*, meaning the 'greater vehicle' and 'lesser or fundamental vehicle' respectively. In essence, Mahāyāna is called the greater vehicle because its expressed aim, in a many-sided approach, is the liberation of *all* beings. Its ideal figure is the *bodhisattva* who, from compassion, postpones his own well-merited entry into Nirvāna until all other beings have realized their absolute nature. Hinayāna, perhaps more realistically, lays emphasis on individual realization, concentrating on monasticism as its principal means for this. It was the Mahāyāna school of Buddhism which reached China, after which it travelled to Korea, Japan and Vietnam. In a somewhat different form, as *Lamaism*, it is also the religion of Tibet and Mongolia. The second school, considering the term Hinayāna to be somewhat pejorative, prefers to be called *Theravāda* ('Teaching of the elders of the order'). The Theravādin version of Buddhism is prevalent in Sri Lanka, Burma, Thailand, Cambodia and Laos.

During the period of Buddha's own teaching (c520–480 BC) Buddhism seems to have flourished mainly in the North-East of India. As a faith it appealed to all castes, not least because all were equally welcomed – something highly unusual at the time. Two factions gradually emerged: strict conservationists who wrote their tradition into the Canon of Scriptures in the Pali language; and innovators who recorded their doctrines in Sanskrit. After the death of Buddha, Buddhist Councils were convened by rival groups to establish the essential content of the sacred texts and principal disciplinary rules. Buddhism continued in India for more than 1,000 years before its virtual disappearance. What it lost within its country of origin has been more than recompensed by its success outside India.

As well as the expansion into South and South-East Asia, there was a Northern movement across the high desert plateaux of Central Asia, especially along the Silk Road into China. Throughout history, cultural, artistic and spiritual influences have been spread by conquest and the expansion of trade; Buddhism was no exception. As a faith, it was to become particularly successful in China, but first it would encounter a system of belief already flourishing there – *Taoism*.

## Taoism

Taoism (pronounced dow-ism) is a name applied to a religion and a number of schools of philosophy. The term 'Taoism' was not used until the Han Dynasty in the 2nd century AD, by which time its main strands of 'belief' had merged into the concept of *Tao* as the unity behind the multiplicity of things.

Taoism is ascribed to Lao-tzu who was born in South China in 604 BC. His name (which means 'wise old child') arose from the legend that he was born an old man. Lao-tzu was an archivist who, wearying of political life, withdrew from society and lived for decades in a hut on the side of a mountain. At 80 years of age he wrote the *Tao Teh Ching*, a 5,000-word treatise on the nature of life in harmony with the universe. The words of the title – *Tao* (way) *Teh* (power, virtue) *Ching* (book) – have caused this philosophy to be known as the 'Way of Virtue' or simply, 'The Tao' (the way). Lao-tzu died in 517 BC.

In summary, he taught that salvation is not

attained by prayer but rather by observance of nature – the natural way. As trees bend with the wind, as rivers follow the path of least resistance, so man must accommodate to the rhythm of existence. 'The great Tao flows everywhere; to yield to it is to be sustained in wholeness'.

The *Tao Teh Ching* regards the Tao as the all-embracing ultimate principle which existed before Heaven and Earth. This, the sempiternal life-force that vivifies the physical world, is unnamable and cannot be described; causing everything to arise, yet not acting. Its power (Teh) is what phenomena receive from Tao, animating them and making them what they are. The goal of the philosophical Taoist is to become one with the Tao by realizing the Universal law of 'the return of everything to its source'. For this, the aspirant must acquire the emptiness (*wu*) and simplicity (*p'u*) of Tao and abide in non-action (*wu-wei*).

> *Empty yourself of everything.*
> *Let the mind rest at peace.*
> *The ten thousand things rise and fall while the*
> *    Self watches their return.*
> *They grow and flourish and then return to the*
> *    source.*
> *The return to the source is stillness – which is the*
> *    way of nature.*

*The way of nature is unchanging.*
*Knowing constancy is insight.*
*Not knowing constancy leads to disaster.*
*Knowing constancy, the mind is open.*
*With an open mind, you will be openhearted.*
*Being openhearted, you will act royally.*
*Being royal, you will attain the divine.*
*Being divine, you will be at one with the Tao.*
*To be at one with the Tao is to be eternal.*
*And though the body dies, the Tao will never*
*    pass away.*

*Tao Teh Ching* (Lao-Tzu)

Taoism shares certain similarities with Buddhism, for example, the insistence that intellect cannot comprehend the Unknowable. Taoism teaches that understanding is not derived from knowledge or theory but by comprehension of what is obvious. Into this prepared ground the first Buddhist missionaries planted their teachings. The Chinese received these tolerantly because the new ideas accorded with their general way of doing things. They had always been practical, moralistic, and not very doctrinaire. They sought peaceful social relations and they permitted diverse points of view. Chinese society was, however, already strongly influenced by another body of ideas – *Confucianism.*

# Confucianism

K'ung-fu-tzu (551–479 BC), anglicized as Confucius, was the founder of the first Chinese wisdom school. According to tradition Confucius was from an impoverished family of the lower nobility. He became a minor government bureaucrat but, perhaps because of his outspokenness, never achieved high office. He developed teachings which became a determining influence on public life in China, Japan and Korea for 2,000 years – until the 20th century.

Confucius believed that good government was fundamentally a matter of ethics. Men must play their assigned roles in a fixed society under authority: 'Let the ruler be a ruler and the subject a subject; let the father be a father and the son a son.' He further believed it to be his task to offer rulers a clear idea of their role and calling, so that they might live up to and accord with the requirements of rulership. To accept the inevitability of the world was one of the outstanding characteristics of the ideal man of Confucius.

Although Confucianism is seen principally as a civic code for achieving an ordered society, its tenets were later practised in such a way that, as a movement, it acquired a quasi-religious character. Between the 3rd and 8th centuries AD, Confucianism was penetrated by teachings of Taoist and Buddhist origin. In

China it continues to be important as a personal philosophy of life.

## Chinese Buddhism

What some historians have called 'the Buddhist conquest of China' and others 'the Chinese transformation of Buddhism', coincided with the beginning of the Christian era. The enterprising Emperor Ming (AD 58–75) is reliably reported to have sent messengers to India requesting Buddhist teachers. In the middle of the second century the Emperor Han was converted and set up an 'office of translations' where scholars could work on and store sacred texts, which were mostly in Sanskrit and Chinese. These translators worked with such remarkable fidelity that in modern times it is still possible to reconstruct, almost literally, lost Sanskrit originals from their Chinese translations.

As Chinese Buddhism developed through the 6th and 7th centuries it began to put down deeper doctrinal roots. Increasing numbers of pilgrims went to India returning with texts, some canonical – others of later schools – and all these works were meticulously translated.

Increasingly from this time, Buddhism established itself as one of the three religions of China (with Taoism and Confucianism). A maxim of the time was

'The *three* religions are *one* religion'. Eventually Buddhism in China separated into two distinct movements. *Ch'an* Buddhism cultivated a mind-transcending meditation. The other developed into a devotional sect which practised the invocation of particular buddhas believed to bring benefits to their supplicants (for example, the Amida cult). It was the development of Ch'an Buddhism which made such an impact on Japan.

## Ch'an

Ch'an is not easy to define but Bodhidharma (c AD 470–543?), who came from India to China in AD 520, described it as 'a special transmission outside the scriptures' in which there is 'no dependence on words and letters'. It is 'direct pointing to reality' with 'seeing into one's nature and attainment of Buddhahood'. Bodhidharma brought with him a tradition providing for the transmission of enlightenment from master to disciple. He also introduced what was, for China, a new type of meditation (*pi-kuan* in Chinese) in which the meditator sits gazing at a blank wall, thus emptying the mind of ideas and thoughts.

Question: 'If I have nothing what should I do?'
Answer:    'Throw it away!'
Teaching: Concept is useless, reality is invaluable.

The teachings that began and evolved in India under-went profound change by being absorbed into the Chinese spiritual milieu. The outcome of this absorp-tion was called *Ch'an*. This name comes from a con-traction of *ch'an-na*, which is the Chinese vocalization of the Sanskrit *dhyāna*, meaning meditation.

The meditative life in China was an existence of hard work and rugged self-reliance. Ch'an, influenced by Taoism, took a stance of opposition to scholarly reliance upon texts and stressed instead, oral instruc-tion. In its love of nature and rustic simplicity, Ch'an was, to some extent, the old Taoist tradition in a new guise, and became a major inspiration for artistic and poetic creativity.

Classic Ch'an is a specifically oral teaching, devel-oped by Hui-neng (AD 637–712) and the great masters of the T'ang period who followed him. A characteris-tic of this mode of instruction can be seen from an example when Hui-neng gave advice to a monk: 'What does your own face look like – the Face you had before you were conceived?'

Hui-neng's 'Original Face' teaching-question is one of the most celebrated of a whole genre of teach-ings, now known as the *kōan* (kō-an) a Japanese term meaning 'public-document'. (In Chinese it was called *kung-an* and in Korean, *kong-an*). The kōan presents a formal structure to the mind but the 'solution' has to go beyond construction. It has to be 'direct, immediate and ordinary'. Essential to the kōan is paradox, that which is beyond thinking, that which transcends the logical or conceptual. The kōan cannot be solved by reason; it requires a leap to another level of comprehension.

The Ch'an school, in which sudden enlightenment may take the place of years of arduous intellectual exercise, is a Chinese influence quite unknown to the Buddhists of India or Central Asia. It entirely suited the Chinese mind, which had always concerned itself with things as they are, rather than with speculation as to how they got like that. So in Ch'an meditation it is not expected that practice will bring to mind something *about* the object, or some revelation *concerning* it. It is rather that by resonance with the wholeness of the object there will be a direct revelation, an instantaneous realization; the focus of attention is mirrored back from the object to the *subject* – you yourself. In these circumstances, one's 'self-nature' is faced and revealed, as it is in the haiku verse-philosophy of Japan. This is the self-nature or Buddha-nature lost to sight when obscured by passion and desire.

A simple example of the 'head' (mind) obscuring the direction of the real is illustrated by the occasion when some Buddhist monks were asked to step attentively on the ground and say what they felt. They described the gravel, the earth, etc. They were amazed when the Master exclaimed 'What! Did you not feel the foot?' They had missed the working surfaces and attention had been dissipated.

Carrying the practice further, the discovery is made that we are able to realize our essential 'self-nature', not as an object among objects – nor as a subject among subjects – but JUST AS IT IS! There is a well-known Ch'an saying: 'Before Ch'an, mountains are mountains and rivers are rivers; during Ch'an, mountains are no longer mountains and rivers are no longer rivers; after Ch'an, mountains are mountains and rivers are rivers.' The change arises from the transformational effect of enlightenment, which is like a higher dimension of awakening. Individuality has disappeared into the emptiness of the conditionless All.

## Emptiness

Because so much misunderstanding has arisen over the Buddhist teaching of 'Emptiness' it may be useful to clarify and explain the principle. A good teacher for this purpose is one of the most important Indian philosophers of Buddhism, Nāgārjuna, founder of the Mādhyamika School. He lived around the 2nd or 3rd century AD. The Sanskrit name of the school alludes to the Middle Way, interpreted by its adherents in relation to the existence or the non-existence of things.

Nāgārjuna's principal achievement was his systematization and deepening of the teaching in the *Prajnāpāramitā-sūtra*. (This is extant only in Chinese.) Nāgārjuna, rather like Socrates, developed a type of dialectic using the process of *reductio ad absurdum* to demolish opponents' propositions. Beginning from the premise that something 'exists' only by virtue of its opposite, he demonstrated that all things are only relative and are without essence. He contended that this essence is eternal, immutable and independent, whereas things in the world of appearance are impermanent. They arise, pass away and so are empty.

The word 'emptiness', *shūnyatā* in Sanskrit, has a three-fold significance for the Mādhyamika School.

1  It is the absence of an essential self in anything which is only relative.
2  It also means 'egolessness'.
3  It means liberation, because the conditionless state of emptiness is synonymous with the absolute. To realize emptiness is to attain liberation, which occurs when affirmation and negation (the opposites which comprise relativity) have been dissolved by purification of mind.

When the ghostly emptiness of the ego is understood and the emptiness of all created things realized, what is left is their essence – Consciousness.

For Nāgārjuna the phenomenal world is

characterized by multiplicity, the basis of all mental representation and thus the appearance of an external world. Absolute reality, on the other hand, is devoid of all manifoldness. It is what lies behind the manifest; still and one – it is *Nirvāna*. (Nirvāna is a Sanskrit word meaning 'extinction'.) For Nāgārjuna, Nirvāna is not something to be attained; it is rather the realization of the true nature of phenomena, known when manifoldness is at rest. It is liberation following the merging of the individual self in Brahman. An essentially practical teacher, Nāgārjuna asserts that in liberation one can operate within the world of duality while recognizing its relativity.

The influence that Buddhism was to have on haiku poetry was moving towards Japan but it first travelled to Korea.

## Korean Buddhism

In the 2nd and 1st centuries BC Korea had been under the aegis of China and had therefore been influenced directly by Chinese Buddhism and Confucianism. In Korea new forms of Confucian thought evolved and a distinctive form of Meditative Buddhism was developed.

The introduction of Buddhism into Korea had followed soon after the spread of that teaching into China in the 4th century AD. At that time, Korea was divided into three independent states, none of which had a culture much above primitive animism. But following the arrival of a Mahāyāna Buddhist monk called Sundo, carrying Buddha images, sacred books and filled with missionary zeal, the three Korean states rapidly absorbed the new religion and its accompanying culture. By the middle of the 6th century AD the King of the South-Western state was sending missionaries, images and books to the Emperor of Japan. It thus came about that Korea served as a bridge for the passage of Buddhism into Japan.

## Shinto

Buddhism was introduced into Japan in the 6th century AD by Korean scholars. At this time the country was still separated into feudal clans. Buddhism was regarded as 'the modern doctrine' by Japanese progressives who used it as a weapon against *Shinto* – the traditional religion practised by the conservative guardians of the feudal order.

The indigenous religion of Japan and the bedrock of its religious experience is *Shinto* ('The Way of the Gods') which consists, very simply, of paying reverence to all things in nature, including one's ancestors. Shinto teaches that all things, animate and inanimate, have their own *kami* (spirits or gods). From earliest times, Shinto emphasized rituals promoting bodily cleanliness and fertility. In modern Japan, sects of Shinto have proliferated and continue to flourish.

## Japanese Buddhism

In AD 588 the Empress Suiko ascended the throne and her nephew, Shōtoku Taishi, an ardent Buddhist, became regent. He sent scholars to China to bring back comprehensive knowledge both of Buddhism and of the Chinese system of government. He built the first public Buddhist temple in Japan and the first monastic school. Exemplifying the humanitarianism of the Mahāyāna, he erected a hospital, a dispensary and a house of refuge. Gradually Buddhism spread outwards from the court and the aristocracy to become the religion of the people.

Gyōgi, a patriarch of the Hosso sect of Buddhists, (AD 667–748) devised a formula for the fusion of Buddhism and Shinto. He did this so successfully that soon the common man was Shintoist and Buddhist simultaneously, experiencing no difficulty in living with the duality.

## Zen

The origins of Zen lay in China with Hui-neng, whose Southern school stressed the doctrine of sudden enlightenment (*tongo*). Another school of Ch'an, the Northern school originated by Shenhsui, taught gradual enlightenment (*zengo*) but survived for only a short time. The lineage of the Southern school had split into several currents within the Ch'an tradition, including two of special importance to Japan. These two traditions (called Rinzai and Sōtō in Japanese) reached Japan in the 12th and 13th centuries respectively. Within China the Ch'an sect is now in decay, but in Japan Zen is still influential and active in the two main transmissions: *Rinzai* (now divided into a number of subsects) and *Sōtō* (to which about two-thirds of Japanese temples belong). Both traditions provide the means for sweeping away preconceived ideas. They emphasize the misleading nature of the concepts with which we try to analyse and understand the world.

*Rinzai*

The founder of Zen in Japan was Eisai (1141–1215), who brought back from China the Rinzai Sect of Zen in 1191. He established its first school of learning, Shofuku-ji near Hakata in Kyūshū. In 1215 he founded the Jufuku-ji monastery at Kamakura which (with Kyōto) became one of the most important centres of Zen in Japan. Eisai is also credited with the introduction of tea to Japan.

Although Rinzai and Sōtō are in agreement on all main teachings, Rinzai emphasizes the importance of the

*Kōan* training device. Ta-hui Tsung-kao, the Rinzai master of 12th century China, had collected many examples of the authentic *kōan* and arranged them into a systematic course of Zen practice (Kanna Zen).

As has been explained, the kōan is an insoluble problem, very like a riddle which baffles the intellect and violates the postulates of logic. A suitable example is prescribed by a Zen master and given to the student at a required interview. Later, when the student feels he has obtained some insight relating to his kōan, he returns to the Master with it during the next meditation period. Because it is inherently paradoxical the kōan will not yield to reason, analysis or logic. The Zen student therefore directs his application to the statement even though he does not know beforehand what he may eventually see. He addresses it with his life, his will, his Zen faith and he does not give up.

The kōan is an artificial device contrived to concentrate the student's powers and jolt him into sudden intuitive enlightenment. In general, kōans contain stories about masters of the golden age of Zen during the T'ang dynasty (AD 618–906). Apart from stories about famous masters, some kōans are simply brief statements expressing a paradoxical idea. Hakuin (1685–1768) in 18th-century Japan devised one of the most famous, the 'sound of one hand'. This is usually extended to 'What is the sound of one hand clapping?' The Tibetan *lama* (religious master), Sogyal Rinpoche

(1980), has described how intelligent monks, although acknowledging that a kōan is designed to be unanswerable, nevertheless produce intellectual responses to their kōans as a diversion. To the question, 'What is the sound of one hand clapping?' his answer was 'One hand *is* sound but it needs the other hand to make it manifest!' He had discovered that the sound of one hand is the sound of sound! There are about 700 such recognized or accepted kōans in Japan.

### Sōtō

Dōgen (AD 1200–1253) introduced the Sōtō Sect to Japan in 1227, and is without question the most important Zen master of Japan. In the Sōtō Sect the emphasis was on *zazen* (sitting in meditation) as a means of attaining *satori* (enlightenment). Although the meditative practices of Sōtō Zen might have made it seem quietistic, its discipline produced rugged individualists who could easily turn to action when required.

To this day Zen students do not study scriptures or listen to lectures under this system. They spend hours, sometimes years, sitting in silent meditation while a fellow monk walks slowly behind the lines of meditators carrying vertically in his hands a flat stick with which to strike the shoulders of anyone who dozes.

The state of spiritual enlightenment sought by Zen

devotees (satori) is the point where, released from the grip of worldly passions and at one with the universe, the life is illuminated. This brings an ability to discern the difference between reality and illusion; between the truth and falsehood. The discipline practised in Zen temples is very strict, and to complete even a few months of such training is a considerable accomplishment.

Reinforced by the powerful practice of sitting meditation (zazen), the spirit of Zen fully manifested in Japan and merged deeply with the religious structure and culture of the country. The history of Japanese painting, poetry and theatre is inseparable from Zen. It is the essence of the Japanese aesthetic in flower arrangement, the tea ceremony, calligraphy and design – and haiku.

The syllable *dō* is the Japanese way of pronouncing the Chinese character for Tao. The Zen way (*dō*) gradually imbued a number of activities with the mind-stilling, meditative spirit characteristic of Zen practice. Among these are:

*kadō* the way of flowers;
*chadō* the way of tea;
*kendō* the way of the sword;
*kyudō* the way of archery;
*jūdō* the way of self-defence;
*shōdō* the way of calligraphy.

Japanese philosophy has not evolved as an abstract conceptual idealism. Rather, it exerts its main thrust within the practising realm of immediate experience. Having received enlightenment, a man still enjoys earthly activity in a life-affirming transformation, freed from the inhibiting effect of the ego. If awareness is total, perception of what is required is accurate and the response full. Conflicting desires need not arise and action will be decisive, immediate and spontaneous. Zen realization is the ultimate extension of religious consciousness – at which extreme it is Absolute.

We shall now consider how it was within this context that concise and essential statements of poetry, imbued with the spirit of Zen, came to be part of Japan's rich and unique culture.

## Japanese Poetry

The question is, how did Japanese poetry in its written form come to have the configuration now recognized as *haiku*?

An 8th-century book, the *Kaifuso*, is an anthology of poetry written in Chinese by Japanese courtiers. The Chinese language was used to demonstrate erudition but also to convey thoughts considered too difficult or extended for the standard Japanese verse-forms.

In contrast the *Manyōshū*, Japan's oldest anthology of verse, contains more than 4,000 poems in Japanese compiled by the poet Yakamochi Ōtōmo, also in the 8th century. It includes some pieces composed as early as the 5th century. The collection contains poetry of many styles, reflecting Japanese life and civilization of the 7th and 8th centuries. It also shows, if only slightly, some influence of Buddhism, Confucianism and Taoism. The poetry was written by men and women of all classes: emperors, members of the nobility and the poorest of common people. It reveals the brightness of city life and the simple charm of the countryside. Many translations are offered even for the title of this compilation, one example being, 'Collection of Ten Thousand Leaves'.

Because in Japanese most words end in one of five vowels, rhymed poetry could tend toward monotony, but by adopting the creative device of alternating five and seven-syllable lines, Japanese poetry has acquired its characteristic rhythm and does not need rhyme to make it interesting. In Japan primitive song and early poetry had evolved through a long period of oral tradition before being written down, and it is difficult to assign precise dates in its history when it acquired a regular form and a fixed syllabic prosody.

In very early songs and poems such as those preserved in the Manyōshū, lines vary in length from three to nine syllables but already there are signs of a preference for five or seven syllables. However, by the time the great majority of the poems in the Manyōshū had been written, song had undergone development into poem and had acquired an established configuration. Eventually, short and long lines (of five and seven syllables) alternated, in due course becoming a poem of 31 syllables in the pattern 5–7–5 and 7–7. This form was called *tanka*, ('short poem') and sometimes *waka*, ('Japanese poem').

The various transitions of poetry, moving through forms such as the *hanka*, *chōka*, *sedōka*, *waka* and *tanka* are a specialist study, but the emergence of the haiku and senryu can be simply explained. (For a fuller treatment of this subject see the author's *Breathing with the Mind*.)

Because tanka (31-syllable poems) contained two components, they eventually separated into discrete poems of 17 and 14 syllables. From this division there emerged a linked-verse form called *haikai-renga* or 'chain-poem', to which many people contributed. Its first main group of 17 syllables constituted a 'header-poem', called *hokku* ('hook'). Some poets, among them Bashō and his pupils, often wrote only the opening lines of a *renga* (verse-linking), dispensing with the rest of the chain. More and more poets followed this practice and, in time, the three lines of 17 syllables came to be considered a poem in its own right. This shorter form was at first called *haikai* and then later, at the end of the 19th century, Masaoka Shiki made the name *haiku* the generic term for this form of poetry.

The haiku consists of 17 syllables or units of sound, arranged in a three-line pattern of 5–7–5. Matsuo Bashō (1644–99) is now considered to be the founder of the classical art of haiku and the greatest Japanese haiku poet. He was an adherent of Zen and practised under the Master Bu'cho. His best haiku, which became models for all later haiku poets, are permeated with the mind of Zen and express its nondualistic experience.

Here is an example of Bashō's work written as he walked near a fishing village:

> *At sunrise I see*
> *Tanned faces of fishermen –*
> *Among white poppies!*

A later haiku, written by Mizuta Masahide (1657–1723) after his storehouse was razed by fire:

> *Kura yakete sawaru mono naki tsukimi kana.*
> *With my barn burned down,*
> *Nothing obstructs my view of*
> *The moon overhead!*

The haiku is free from the rules and restrictions which bind orthodox waka but it does have canons of good taste – unwritten rules to which its votaries conform with common consent. For example, a true haiku should be a simple and direct expression (sometimes an exclamation) of pure response to a glimpse or scene in life, with no intervention from logical intellect. The good haiku is a picture in words, rich in suggestiveness – not an explanation or argument. It is a somewhat formal and spare statement reflecting nature and the seasons. Its severity suggests that the ego-reflecting mirror in the poet has been shattered by a Zen-like impact, leaving unobscured that universal mirror which reflects the Natural World. From the poem's austerity it should not be assumed that writers of these verses had an unrelenting or dour outlook – far from it. Humour, irony, wit and realism were prominent. Moreover, with Bashō came aesthetic values hitherto unknown to haiku – a wistful austere beauty (*sabi*) and a seeming naivety and lightness of touch (*karumi*). Pervading Japanese culture and its poetry are four moods which are very difficult to define: a sadness for the transience of natural things (*aware*); loneliness welcomed as detachment – (a further dimension of *sabi*); the 'suchness' of ordinary things (*wabi*); and the mysterious strangeness in profundity (*yugen*). There is, too, the concept *shibui*: in translation 'austere, subdued, restrained', but to the Japanese suggesting also quietness, depth, purity, simplicity and, in a positive sense, reticence.

The haiku is separated into two components by *kareji* (cutting words) which also produce a pause in the rhythmic flow. The verse is usually cut after five syllables but it may be at the end of the seven-syllable line, as in this celebrated haiku by the master Bashō:

> *On a withered bough*
> *A solitary crow sits –*
> *Autumn evening.*

Sometimes *kareji* will be an exclamation to direct attention, as in this verse by Issa:

> *Oh! unseemly breeze –*
> *Thatcher at work on the roof*
> *I can see your rump!*

The warmth of the Japanese people prompted them to seek another vehicle to express, in a more relaxed way, their wry observations on the human condition. Accordingly a more liberal, parallel pattern of 17 syllables called the *senryu* gradually came into being. This verse-form, composed by people from all walks of life, reached maturity in Edo (now Tokyo) under Karai Senryu (1718–1790) whose name it now bears. This is, in form, a haiku but it satirizes human foibles and allows the poet much more freedom of content. An example of each demonstrates the difference:

first a haiku:

> *Sun setting, autumn*
> *Quietness – a stag's bellow*
> *Echoes from the hills.*

now a senryu:

> *Crockery cupboard*
> *Empty, sink completely full –*
> *His wife is away!*

To summarize the difference, a *haiku* expresses a moment of insight into the world of nature; a *senryu* is a satirical statement on the nature of the world.

Some 18th-century purists deprecated the senryu characteristics creeping into haiku, but both forms have continued in popularity with the ordinary people. The impact of Bashō and Senryu on Japanese poetry was that of a new influence on a flourishing, centuries-old art form. The poetry written by the Japanese Imperial Court between AD 550 and 1350 constitutes one of the great literary genres of the world. Among the leisured classes, personal communication often took the form of an exchange of poems. Poetry was also a serious and important detail of courting activity between couples. The 31 syllable poems sent by a lover were scrutinized carefully for poetic fluency and the quality of the calligraphy.

During the 9th century in court circles, poetry contests became widespread and remained popular over the next 100 years. Down the centuries one of the more enjoyed events of the New Year in Japan has been the poetry-reading party. In modern times the most distinguished is that held by the Emperor and Empress at the Imperial Palace to celebrate the New Year, known as *Uta Kai Hajimae* ('First Poetry Reading'). In conjunction with this, there is an annual national poetry competition which attracts well over 30,000 entries.

> *This year's first poem*
> *Achieved with self confidence –*
> *A haiku master.*
>
> Buson (1716–1783)

The haiku and senryu which appear in the main section of this present volume are English originals written by the author specifically for this book. The verses, imbued with the spirit of the Japanese experience, are relevant to life today. They are not in sequence or grouped by subject because each is a complete statement intended to stand alone.

A good haiku, once heard, stays in the memory. Haiku and senryu create a word-picture full of implications and understated significance. Their brevity makes them difficult to write well but this is the challenge which has made the haiku one of the most popular forms in the history of poetry. A celebrated maxim of Tokugawa Ieyasu asserts that 'The insufficient is better than the superfluous'. In this there is no question of lack or limitation; haiku and senryu perfectly exemplify the Eastern axiom 'less is more' and they do it by potent understatement. There is a confidence and a generosity in their very compactness which arise from the Japanese attitude to life and things.

Despite its deceptive simplicity the haiku is a sophisticated literary morsel, subtle and stimulating but drawing on the reader's own experience to augment what is presented. This has a two-fold effect: an evocative image connects the reader to universal experience – then beauty and insight produce an instantaneous awakening! The understatement in the haiku is expanded by experience in the reader, who thus contributes to the creative act. Some verses are fleeting glimpses noted in passing; others have a profundity consonant with the deeper realms of philosophy. At both levels we are offered a fresh perspective on life and relationships.

To conclude, the haiku is Zen-inspired verse philosophy – very stylized and very Japanese. Yet Zen is wholly a Chinese derivation from Buddhism and Buddhism originated in India within the fertile milieu of Hinduism. All these resonances await discovery

packed into the brevity of the haiku and senryu which
follow; they will yield to your exploration . . .

# Haiku and Senryu
# Verses and Notes

⟡

*Awakening to*
*The awareness beyond mind –*
*Only now is real.*
        Shinri (1931– )

*Cold, bright, symmetry,*
*Glistening in the sunlight –*
*Resplendent Fuji.*

Tiny and perfect,
Abundant in this damp ditch –
The new season's frogs!

Allowing yourself
To be drawn gently within –
Enter meditation . . .

Bees gather honey
Wasps just fly around – who are
We to criticize?

*Peering out through our*
*Eye-windows, pretending that*
*We are inside ourselves.*

*He, discovering*
*The nature of love in her*
*Gift – giving himself . . .*

*An intention to*
*Empty the mind obstructs*
*Entry into 'no-mind'.*

The Zen state of 'no-mind', a much valued condition, occurs when ego is not present. Purposeful intent to bring this about is an ego-driven desire which blocks the way. During meditation, the state of 'no-mind' opens to one who has surrendered desire and anticipation of experience.

44

*Habits are like clothes*
*Long ago worn out, but still*
*Adorning vagrants.*

*Religion, ever*
*Maintaining duality*
*And separation!*

*Volitional acts –*
*Imply ego 'doing' in*
*Response to desire.*

To know, without the
Knowing, is to realize
The 'suchness' of things.

Society, with
Its ritual posturing, –
These mating pigeons!

Mountains, valleys, 'Ten
Thousand Things' all expressing –
Natural true Self.

*Human beings,*
*Each learning what is needed for life –*
*Wasting what is known . . .*

*Making mistakes is*
*A natural process – but*
*Make them only once!*

*Asked 'How should I live?'*
*The Zen master succinctly*
*Said 'Go straight; don't know!'*

To a major question the Zen master gives a vastly comprehensive answer in small compass, neatly turning concept into precept.

*'I love you so much*
*It hurts' she said, welcoming*
*Life's favourite pain.*

*A suburban fox,*
*Minding its own business*
*Trots quietly by . . .*

*The 'not-knowing' of*
*Knowing, is non-conceptual*
*Knowledge of being.*

Take it slowly! This apparent conundrum is indicating the difference between conceptual knowledge in space-time and the perceptive knowing which stems from being aware that I-am.

*Clarifying the*
*Mind first – then perceiving the*
*True nature of things.*

*Greater intelligence –*
*Implies capacity for*
*Deeper ignorance!*

*True 'emptiness' is*
*Like deep sleep without dreaming –*
*Your real self is there.*

In ancient India Buddhism was so popular that Hindu teachers, including Shankara, mounted a campaign against it. Accordingly they derided and condemned the teaching of 'Emptiness', misrepresenting it as a vacuum. In truth, like Hinduism's own Advaita teaching, 'Emptiness' means that the Natural World (*prakriti* in Sanskrit) can only react mechanically and is totally dependent on the all-pervading Consciousness (*purusha*).

*Her sweet voice always*
*Delights – but her whispers are*
*A special music!*

*The student asked his*
*Real question – the teacher*
*Gave his false answer.*

This verse alludes to the limited pedagogue, not the spiritual Master Teacher.

*Breathtaking in her*
*Magnificent remote grace –*
*The geisha walking . . .*

The geisha is a highly accomplished singer, dancer and instrumentalist. Impeccably mannered, professional and well-informed, she is also a brilliant conversationalist. Geisha are generally highly regarded and often marry into good families.

Menacingly, the
Heron peering down – suddenly
Becomes a spear.

*After this life ends*
*The journey is a long one –*
*Better change our clothes!*

*'I can't work miracles!'*
*He rants now – but earlier*
*He believed he could.*

*Two monks rolling up*
*Bamboo blinds in the same way –*
*One gains, one loses.*

The Zen master pointed to the bamboo blinds and two monks immediately went over and rolled them up, simultaneously and identically. The master remarked, 'One gains, one loses'. Can you see why?

There are many meanings in this teaching story. One monk did it for a result, the other did not; one was merely the agent for the action, the other *did* it personally; one was obedient to direction, the other volitionally performed a service; one merely witnessed the action without attachment, the other observed it from personality.

Swans, white and silent,
Glide as if meditating –
Snow-drifts on water.

Mindless, the scarecrow
Stands guard in the field; the birds
Uncertain, furtive.

Just your being there –
The essential delight of
Existence, here, now.

Elusive cuckoo –
Heard not seen! Are you a bird
  Or merely a voice?

Sunlit snow melting –
At the roof edge poised, glistening
  Drops ready to drip.

The clapping of one
Hand manifesting as sound –
  Hearing the silence!

This *kōan* directs us past the obviousness of sensory experience to the subtlety of insight.

Sheltering from the
Rain, the shop's contents
  Noted with disinterest.

Her giving seeming
To her no longer enough –
  Discovering love.

For a thousand years,
Breathing your message of
  Transience – summer breeze.

*Killing a rumour –*
*Like trying to cover a*
*Hundred empty pots.*

*Where the servant is*
*Without pay, the master must*
*Be without anger.*

*The spinning-wheel of*
*The widow, like the glutton's*
*Mouth – never at rest.*

This senryu disturbs by the apparent incongruity of juxta-
posing the widow's necessity with the glutton's excess. The
restlessness in both situations represents an imbalance in
society.

Merely pronouncing
The word 'sugar' creates no
Sweetness on the tongue.

A crack in the wall –
But to the beetle inside
It is a mansion.

The surly peasant,
Sitting grumbling at the cow –
As he takes her milk.

An insidious
Power ploy; the 'holier
Than thou' attitude!

Murky water, but
Perfectly reflecting the moon's
Radiance – stillness.

Love is not blind; but
Desire unfortunately,
Usually is!

*Holding the mirror*
*Of life to my face, I see –*
*Experience.*

The peacock, merely
Displaying; it's we who think
'Proud' and 'beautiful'.

'Let's make up and be
Friends' he said, preparing for
His next big assault.

Why do you assume
That eyes brimming with tears are
Mere manipulation?

Tears are often believed to be a device or an escape route
but are usually a natural and genuine reaction.

*Volition faltering;*
*Could this be egoism*
*Succumbing to love?*

*Slavery has not*
*Been abolished; we simply*
*Call it something else!*

*Telling him what he*
*Ought to think and feel, she rapes*
*His integrity.*

'I know better' is an insidious arrogance. Suggestion, reasoning, advising from knowledge, are not the same as verbal aggression.

*What use is it to*
*Turn the other cheek – but then*
*Harbour resentment?*

*The receptive is*
*Yielding; no reason for it*
*To be otherwise.*

*His resistance to*
*Saying 'I love you' is more*
*Than simple shyness!*

Some people find it impossible to express their feelings –
even to say a simple 'thank you'.

*That flash of lightning!*
*Bright, but of brief duration –*
*Like human pleasure.*

*Mediocrity,*
*Masquerading as being*
*Nice to everyone!*

*As two merge into*
*One, both egos dissolving*
*In accord – love grows . . .*

Striving to conform
To the expectations of
Others – missing life.

The tied sack safeguards
Its contents; the human mouth
Spills words everywhere.

On its hind legs, a
Performing dog imitates
Man – how like ego!

*Beyond everything*
*Lies conceptual freedom –*
*How will you reach it?*

*Mismanaged aggression –*
*Slowly degenerating*
*Into depression.*

*Preparing for his*
*Visit, no detail is too*
*Much trouble – her love!*

*Obsession controls*
*An underlying wish – look*
*At the wish itself.*

*'Always' and 'Never'*
*Keep appearing when he speaks;*
*Surely, he's not divine?*

These generalizing absolute words are rarely appropriate in ordinary conversation; it is Truth which is omniscient, all-pervading, never changing . . .

*An intuitive*
*Looking into the nature*
*Of things – satori!*

Degrees of satori range from a glimpse of intuitive understanding to total Enlightenment. As D T Suzuki said, 'The opening of satori is the remaking of life itself'.

Civilization –
Cultural development
Or stifler of life?

Human sourness; a
Lemon, minus the joy of
Yellow and fragrance.

As I am special
I'm not surprised that other
People seem so dull!

It is not always appreciated that being 'special' is a severe
limitation and it might be just a private idea.

*Plum-blossom, perceived*
*Transient perfection – are*
*You witnessing us?*

*Human rituals –*
*Substitute for meaningful*
*Relationships.*

*Passively expressed*
*As nonresponsiveness – her*
*Silent resentment.*

*He only believes*
*He's Napoleon – some are*
*Claiming to be God!*

*Demolished by her*
*Good sense, in desperation*
*He starts to bluster.*

*Gesture intended*
*To stir conscience in someone*
*Else – the suicide.*

*'I hear what you say'*
*He said as he resolutely*
*Closed his mind's ear.*

*'If God should ever*
*Require a helping hand, He*
*Only has to ask . . . '*

*Examining the*
*Import of experience –*
*The philosophers.*

*Reaching towards true*
*Being, beyond time and space –*
*Meditating mind . . .*

In the practice of meditation, gradually one learns to let go of the everyday busy conditioned self to discover the innate natural self. By releasing and relaxing we come 'home' to ourselves. It is like finding blue sky behind the clouds, as we discover the true being which is spacious and clear.

*Bedraggled sheep*
*Waiting with total indifference –*
*The incessant rain!*

*Not only in France*
*Is rapprochement of egos*
*Mistaken for love!*

*A green woodpecker*
*Is resting its head, eating*
*Ants from the greensward . . .*

The staccato drumming which accompanies the woodpecker's feasts at the woodland trees is silent while he eats at a softer table . . .

*Exaggerating*
*As usual he shouts 'You've*
*Got it upside down!'*

*Gazing with wonder –*
*The baby looking at quite*
*Ordinary things.*

*Warm honeysuckle*
*Fragrant with scent, yet the bees*
*Seem indifferent.*

Nature implants drives, but we human beings seem to expect instinctive creatures to enjoy them like us.

*The cult's aim is to*
*Destroy ego but the leader's*
*Own is flourishing!*

*This toddler, reaching*
*Out to touch, exercising*
*Its future grasping . . .*

*Blossom and songbirds –*
*'Radiance' and 'melody'*
*Are mental concepts!*

It is not necessary to conceptualize simple perceptions.
When the head dominates responses it produces a mentally
structured substitute for the real world.

*Looking as if it*
*Will sit for eternity*
*Right there – an old frog.*

*People ask questions –*
*Seeking answers that confirm*
*Only what they know.*

*In a stone there is*
*Mountain; a splash of water*
*Signifies the sea.*

The nature of things is discovered in details; the essence reveals the whole.

*The baby's soft gaze;*
*Unsophisticated and*
*Open – free of guile.*

*Thrusting from below*
*Everywhere, like tips of spears –*
*Spring bulbs surfacing.*

*In the brief pauses*
*Between successive actions –*
*Glimpse eternity.*

A momentary pause in the space between successive actions allows a decoupling from spent force, preventing the exhaustion of obsessiveness. This practice offers a moment of rest in which time does not exist.

Meditation is
What happens when the doing
Becomes witnessing.

Spontaneously
Aware in the moment now –
Why come back to time!

Japanese surgeon,
Lifting a single grain of
Rice with his chopsticks!

Observed during his meal, this skilled practitioner cannot resist an opportunity to exercise precision.

Voices of insects,
Wind-blown grasses whispering –
I am listening . . .

*For a fine horse it*
*Will have been enough, merely*
*To have glimpsed the whip.*

*Fissures everywhere*
*Snorting like dragons' nostrils –*
*Volcanic Japan.*

The coastal area of Beppu is one of Japan's active areas of hot springs and rising plumes of scalding water-vapour. The land breathes clouds!

*If everything has*
*Its price, with what will you redeem*
*Your colossal debt?*

Everything is given or lent to us while we are alive – even the air we breathe is free.

*In your strait-jacket,*
*Maintaining the 'Me-concept' –*
*Individual!*

*Heard just at twilight,*
*The thin pipe of a robin –*
*Time to meditate . . .*

*Objects perceived by*
*Eyes alone – are no more than*
*Representation!*

Appearances everywhere are projected by the mind upon an energy system of sub-atomic particles in continuous and eternal motion – a world of relativity which is a mere representation of the Ultimate Reality's absolute permanence.

*Aligned along the*
*Bare thread of meditation –*
*Meditating mind. . .*

*Preoccupied, deep*
*Within our private world – a*
*Darkness without the stars!*

*I do help others –*
*(When it does not interfere*
*With my private life).*

Grudgingly, like a miser opening his purse, we extend ourselves towards others.

*If you have left 'now'*
*To look at the future,*
*    You have played with death!*

*Showers in April;*
*Intensive, but not lasting –*
*    Like men's promises.*

*Experiencing*
*Witnessed by pure consciousness –*
*    Knowledge arising. . .*

*Anxiety – from*
*Suppression of her feelings*
*Of low self-esteem.*

*Reaching towards the*
*Ultimate reality –*
*Mind meditating . . .*

*Creative process*
*And swift path to misery –*
*Imagination!*

The ability to visualize has the capacity to destroy or to liberate – guard the mind!

Pushing against a
Door that is not really there –
His wooing of her.

*When an inner smile*
*Permeates the body – it*
*Emits radiance!*

*Acorns or people –*
*Such abundance; Nature is*
*Never miserly.*

*If you learn to die*
*Before you die, then when you*
*Die you will not die.*

The ego 'dies' each night in deep sleep. It stirs fitfully during
dreaming sleep and emerges fully when awakening occurs.
Because the ghostly ego, the 'me-concept', does not really
exist we could let it die now!

The mantra, like a
Mountain stream, purifying
Whoever chants it.

'One goes through people'
She complained, symbolizing
The consumer age.

Harmony, created
By life expressing itself –
Old Kyōto!

Kyōto has a long history. Its original grid-pattern of streets, temples, shops and waterways are harmonious, having evolved to meet the needs of its human inhabitants. Suchness is rightness!

*Death – the ultimate
Transition in a life of
Constant becoming.*

*That to which you have
Chosen to give attention –
Your experience.*

*Living can take place
By itself – YOU are free to
Witness being lived.*

We often 'push the river' assuming that we are 'responsible',
that we have to 'do' everything that happens. Without that
assumption, ego would be redundant and we would become
the witnessing audience.

*Ghostly images*
*Without substantiality –*
*Imagination.*

*'I'm only human!'*
*Is the diminishing bleat*
*Of bruised self-esteem.*

We tend to under-estimate our potential at less-inspired moments. The limits of human achievement are unknown because they have not yet been reached!

*Caprice is not the*
*Expression of freedom, but*
*A despotic act.*

It is not only feudal emperors who oppress with absolute power. Even a child mistreating something living and helpless behaves like a despot.

*'Service of others'*
*Is sometimes an excuse to*
*Exploit devotion.*

*That child needs help,*
*But most of the adults are*
*Always so busy!*

*Being the subject*
*We could not be an object*
*Of contemplation.*

The individual confuses the 'one' of individuality with the 'One' of unity. Each ego perceives itself as at the centre of everything simply because it has a 'separate' point of view. There is only one moon overhead, but it is reflected in myriad oceans, lakes and puddles. The mirrored images are *objects* but the moon itself is the *subject* of its countless reflections. Without this grammar of duality, we could transfer our allegiance to the real source of light and realize THAT.

*Transmuting his breathed*
*Music into Zen – the*
*Shakuhachi player.*

The history of the *shakuhachi* is a curious one. In the 17th century, the freedom of the *samurai* warrior class was curtailed. Forbidden to carry weapons, resourceful masterless samurai redesigned the bamboo flute, strengthening it to serve as a weapon while also providing them with a livelihood as musicians. With their heads concealed inside wicker basket hats, the *komuso* (as these flute-playing beggar-priests were called) wandered the streets, developing the art of the shakuhachi. Eventually the government of the day recognized them as a religious sect but, in return, required them to act as spies. Komuso can still be found in modern Tokyo but many people believe that what they see and overhear under their basket hats is passed on to the police. In contrast to their earlier history, the modern shakuhachi player has a respected place at recitals and on the professional concert platform. This profoundly soulful music is often associated with the spiritual atmosphere of Zen meditation.

*A creation is*
*Perfect exactly at the*
*Point of completion.*

*Good health is often*
*A balancing act – so what*
*Turns at the pivot?*

*The great within the*
*Small – principle expressing*
*Hidden potential.*

While there is a great force within the atom, it must also
be remembered that you cannot get a quart into a pint pot!

*The piquant sweet smell*
*Of woodsmoke in the nostrils –*
*Night's lodging is near.*

'Leave it with me' he
Said, with discouragingly
Dissuasive coldness.

Long ago, humans
Developed speech; what is it
Being used for now?

Such a mournful cry
Despite the pomp and dazzling
Plumage – the peacock.

When will the sound we make match our splendid adorn-
ment – we are human beings!

*The new-born baby –*
*Separate but not yet an*
*Individual.*

*That special moment*
*On first waking – soon to be*
*Lost in day-dreaming.*

*'Let me do it for*
*You' she said, thus ensuring*
*Growing dependence.*

Often the waning powers of the elderly are subverted by assertive appropriation of the little that is left to them.

*This baby, clenching*
*And unclenching fists and toes –*
*Celebrating life!*

*Complete liberation*
*From the world of change –*
*The supreme freedom.*

*Interpretation –*
*Death of the spontaneous*
*Natural response.*

*Perceptive poet;*
*Priest of the invisible –*
*Revealing the truth.*

*Orientation*
*Pointing to reality –*
*Reason's discernment.*

*The man who attacks*
*A woman has contravened*
*A natural law.*

The bullying man who misuses his power, physically or
psychologically against a woman, betrays both himself and
the universal male principle.

*Having no other*
*Employment, her mind invents*
*New apprehensions.*

*His fear of failure*
*Is turning hesitation*
*Into disaster.*

*Fearing ridicule*
*He has attracted just that –*
*By his own clowning.*

Clowning and intrusive joking are often a sad and unsuccessful attempt to win approval from others.

*Wide-eyed, owls can seem*
*Wise; but dozing gently they*
*May fall down chimneys!*

The author rescued a hungry, crest-fallen Brown Owl from his fire-place beneath a tall chimney. From the window it flew off into the copse, probably none the wiser!

*Low-angled wintry*
*Sun, not yet warm enough to*
*Tempt spring buds open.*

*You have a ghostly*
*Lodger lurking in your mind –*
*It is the ego.*

*'Woman' he said, 'is*
*A goddess or a doormat.'*
*Nothing in between?*

This remark, made in fact by Picasso, is a perceptive but woefully simplistic categorization; an attitude of bullying machismo, revealing a fearful deep doubt about maleness.

*When the dragon of*
*Fear is examined it is*
*Found to be a mouse.*

*In this biting east*
*Wind, two doves sit huddled on*
*The branch – they seem sad.*

*Pandering to his*
*Ego, students retard the*
*Teacher's own progress.*

In many cults, the vulnerability of the leader to egoism is not respected by some followers, who offer an unworthy pseudo-acknowledgement of his greatness.

*A false assumption –*
*Two stages of error made*
*For the wrong reason.*

*'My child shall have the*
*Best money can buy!' Fine, and*
*Discipline is free.*

*So then, 'where was your*
*Face before you were conceived?' –*
*The mind has no answer.*

This ego-shattering question, asked by a Zen master of his disciple, has become one of the most celebrated kōans in the canon. Can you answer the question?

*Dry brown leaves swirling –*
*Their susurrous sound softly*
*Whispering 'Autumn'.*

*Carefully keeping*
*Her self to herself, remaining*
*A 'private' person.*

*'I can because I*
*Do' said the able old man,*
*Using his vigour.*

Some people are too willing to give up what has not yet
been taken from them by time.

*Long shadows cast by*
*Old sins, dispersing in the*
*Light of forgiveness. . .*

*'Please yourself' often*
*Means that someone has lost their*
*Influence over you.*

*If today was like*
*Yesterday, you already know*
*About tomorrow!*

If you want to see into the future, observe your habits today; people change slowly if they change at all.

*Choosing plain words*
*To express simple thoughts –*
*Children growing up.*

*The years have piled up*
*Snow on his head; it will have*
*To melt in due course!*

*Memory – the mind's*
*Careful store of selected*
*Past experience.*

Memory with equal precision stores treasure and lumber.
We should learn to discriminate the difference!

*Beyond everything*
*Yet closer than insight –*
*Your natural self.*

*The lessons of birth*
*And death are dispensed by a*
*Harsh tutor – called 'Life'.*

*Multiplicity*
*Having a single source, needs*
*No relationships.*

The philosophy behind this verse is simple but perhaps not apparent to everyone. Within unity everything is already at one with itself; no bridging relationships are necessary. It is like two lovers trying to relate to each other directly instead of being as one through the unifying process of Love.

*Predators wait for
Me outside the hot hell of
My mosquito net.*

It is a great temptation to put one's face outside the moist heat being endured under the mosquito net to feel the cool autumn breeze.

*The complexity*
*Of scholarship gradually*
*Gives way to understanding.*

*The greatest craftsman*
*Has worked on himself first – and*
*On his skills second.*

*The mirror which is*
*Eternal gathers no dust –*
*Yet reflects nothing!*

A mirror reflects images of things. These appearances hide reality, which is the infinite intelligence beyond perception, thought and appearance. Reality is no thing. It is available by direct experience but gives rise to no reflection and casts no shadow.

*That which is perfect*
*Cannot be seen, so you may*
*As well stop looking!*

*Thought has limits but*
*Intelligence is spirit –*
*Which is limitless.*

*The mind of Tao is*
*Quiescent and does not move –*
*Nature does not think!*

A Taoist teaching (*Tao Teh Ching*) says:

All things are together in action,
But I look into their non-action;
For things are continuously moving, restless,
Yet each is proceeding back to its origin.
Proceeding back to the origin means Quiescence;
To be in Quiescence is to see 'being-for-itself'.

*Prodigal water-wheel –*
*Carelessly spilling silver*
*In the sunlight!*

*True emptiness – the*
*Ability to transcend*
*The world's transience.*

*My body is in*
*Its autumn – a leathern bag*
*Not without creases!*

*The world's finest tea*
*Needs a little clear water*
*To express itself.*

*Having absolute*
*Nature, how are you hindered*
*From being yourself?*

*Our true nature is*
*Hidden by a mask we wear –*
*Personality.*

The Greek word *persona* means 'mask', and we actors all have an appearance from behind which we perform on the stage of life. Many people think that we *are* our personality; others believe we have a true essence behind the accretion of skills, social graces and attitudes acquired since birth.

*The moon shines fully*
*Once a month, but disappears*
*Every four weeks!*

*The village below*
*Has disappeared in evening*
*Mist – time to go home.*

*Finding that you have*
*A shiny gold coin, will you*
*Hoard it or spend it?*

With money, we can spend some and save some. But life is for living, and between the extremes is the important principle of using something without consuming it to extinction.

As the child wails at
The top of its shrill voice – its
Mother gives in.

At the point of our
Conception our mothers seem
Quite heedless of us!

'Inner' and 'outer'
Are just ideas – so where
Do you hide yourself?

Her doll becoming,
In play, a younger sister –
The lonely child.

Mind concentrated,
Beads passing through his fingers –
The old jewel-thief.

Turning and tumbling
In the strong wind, like folded
Black paper – the crow.

*The hare leaps and turns*
*Dementedly – is this love*
*Or merely madness?*

*'I can tell my child*
*Anything, he'll believe it' –*
*Betraying adult!*

*The composer worked*
*At the music – performers*
*Will sweat playing it!*

This senryu is questioning 'What is work and what is play in life?' Children play while they learn; are we adults missing something?

*The Noh mask strangely*
*Alive, yet known to be just*
*A face of carved wood.*

Mediocrity
Is comfortable – only
  While you are asleep.

The point at which the
Inward breath turns outward; that
  Is where you are.

An oak tree lives in
The heart of an acorn – what
  Lives within your heart?

*Breath caresses your*
*Life – yet still you refuse to*
*Surrender yourself!*

*What is at the still*
*Point of the turning world? – Not*
*That which has to ask!*

*Serving another –*
*Dissolved separation expressed*
*As a bowl of tea!*

The Tea Ceremony is the central activity in Chadō the 'Way of Tea'. It brings together the artistry of pottery, flower arranging and architecture in a unique tradition. From its ancient origins in Taoism to its culmination in Zen discipline, this elegant and simple ceremony has brought delight to the senses, calm to the mind and refreshment to the spirit.

While eating, become
The tasting of taste – nourish
Yourself with your Self.

Coming to the end
Of something is a false 'stop'
Devised by the mind.

To see everything
As if for the first time – is
To discover life.

If you received the
Innermost secret of life,
    Then what would you do?

When the mind wanders
Where does it go? – Into the
    Past or the future!

Ignorance is what
Follows from thinking you know
    The purpose of life.

If your body is
Really yours, why don't you stop
It growing older?

*You are now somewhere*
*Between birth and death – have you*
*A destination?*

*Derelict wooden*
*Boat, half-submerged among the*
*Rushes – you were new once!*

*If you could halt thinking,*
*Stop talking and cease moving –*
*You could start to live.*

This verse seems to be asking for the impossible but it alludes to circling associative thought, the 'voice in the head' incessantly verbalizing and the ceaseless twitching of a restless body. Life is something else.

*'I learn something new*
*Each day'. he said – but he is*
*Simply catching up!*

*Doubt is often just*
*Laziness – confirmation*
*Abounds everywhere.*

*Tranquillity in*
*Contemplation beyond thought –*
*Deep in samādhi.*

Samādhi (a Sanskrit word) is advanced meditation; a poised active conscious looking without any thinking – simple wholeness occurring by grace after a deep meditation.

Come into balance
Know that you exist here NOW –
Where were you before?

The radiance of
Existence is nothing less
Than your own presence!

Shell picked up on the
Shore of the South China Sea –
JUST another shell?

Tree laden with his
Surplus precious pears – he won't
Give any away.

If the crevices
Of the moon seem mysterious –
Examine your self!

Wild geese driving their
Straight lines across the sunset –
Unreal beauty!

This scene, if painted, would seem too contrived, too
beautiful to be true.

*Some do not reach it*
*Others go well beyond it –*
*The appropriate.*

*In the mirror I*
*See sixty years; in Nature*
*I see it is Spring!*

*Much human learning*
*Is painfully acquired, yet*
*Knowledge is innate.*

Whereas learning is often the laborious assimilation of information, knowledge arises simultaneously with experience.

Creation is a
Continuity – results
 Are just an idea.

A cloud of gnats
Rising and falling at dusk –
 How aware are they?

Freedom is not a
State – it is the 'space' in which
 States are established.

Punishing yourself
Uses up the last few drops
Of your self-esteem.

Ritualistic
Repetitive behaviour –
Call it compulsion!

'How can we be sure?'
She said, injecting doubt and
Irresolution.

*The translator – so*
*Tempted to edge the meaning*
*Towards HIS thinking.*

*Wanting disclosure*
*Of true feelings – but with her*
*Rejection prepared!*

*How do children have*
*All those mood changes without*
*Lasting resentment?*

Adults have well-developed egos and long memories – with this equipment, harbouring resentment is not difficult. Children live for the moment.

One can only learn
From one who knows – you live with
This all-knowing one!

Attention, the eye
Of the will, discerns what you
Have resolved to see.

To speak the truth, one
Must first know what the truth is –
Truth precedes knowledge.

If you do not understand this you have made a useful start.
Press home the question 'What am I?' and the truth will
manifest itself in the detachment of awareness.

*Green haze on winter*
*Twigs – foliage will not wait*
*For the calendar!*

*Hands caressing skin,*
*An unspoken transmission*
*In body-language.*

*Sitting on a small*
*Black cushion facing the wall –*
*Letting go of 'my' world.*

Just sitting (*zazen*) allows the mind to empty of thoughts, such as the 'me-concept' and attachment to 'I-me-mine'. The freedom is delicious, although at the time the 'experiencer' is absent.

*'Being a success'*
*Depends upon who defines*
*It and at what cost.*

*'It's now or never'*
*He says, anticipating*
*Some encouragement.*

*The professional –*
*Qualified yet forever*
*Working in practice!*

*The breath integrates*
*Different levels of being –*
*Into life's wholeness.*

*Unheeded scraps dropped*
*By an elephant nourish*
*A whole nest of ants.*

*'Call no man master' –*
*The preliminary move*
*Towards unity.*

Everyone in ordinary life needs a teacher until the realization that the universal Self is your master. From that absolute position, you can operate within the world of duality while recognizing its relativity.

*Fear is a ghost that*
*Haunts the darker recesses*
*Of the human mind.*

*Drifting may feel good –*
*But with no power, you are*
*Unable to steer!*

*Do emotional*
*And physical states follow*
*The breathing rhythms?*

For centuries 'mindfulness of the breath' has been a technique for heightening awareness. Even in the West we are enjoined to 'take a deep breath' before we react.

*Scriptural precepts*
*May substitute for lack of*
*Natural wisdom.*

*A volitionless*
*Spontaneous release – the*
*Zen archer's arrow.*

*Made to open her*
*Eyes – finding intensity*
*Enhanced to new heights.*

In the moments of ecstasy before surrender, closed eyes deprive the experiencer of an important additional avenue of stimulus.

'The leopard cannot
Change its spots' they say – why on
Earth should it want to?

A *favourable*
Terrain in itself constitutes
Opportunity.

There is no penance
More effective than a spell
Of enforced patience.

Examples abound – for instance, when a bone in the body has been broken, the healing process exacts a charge of sufferance.

*Incomparably*
*Elegant, gliding to her*
*Next meeting – the geisha.*

*Hoping to recoup*
*His losses – the lure that tempts*
*The cardplayer on.*

*Resigned to the rain,*
*Plodding the pace of his beasts –*
*The grumbling cowherd!*

Rain or shine, cows will not be hurried – nor will some people!

*The perceived guru*
*Was discovered to be but*
*A human being.*

Disillusionment with modern gurus is widespread. Blind devotion, unreasoning acceptance, lack of commonsense – all allow the merely extraordinary to appear divine.

*Safely qualified,*
*Glad he's not sitting this*
*Year's Finals papers.*

*The cow, filthy with*
*Winter mire, delivering*
*Its pristine white milk.*

*Do you think that a*
*Millionaire's ego might be*
*Bigger than your own?*

If the ego is still central to thinking, feeling and being, its dimension is of no more relevance than the size of shoes you wear!

*'What happened?' he asked,*
*Surveying the results of*
*His crass carelessness.*

*The best objects and*
*People inevitably*
*Have imperfections.*

It is unrealistic to expect normal things or people to be
ideal.

*The perfect includes –*
*It doesn't reject what YOU*
*Happen to dislike.*

'That is perfect. This is perfect. Perfect comes from
perfect. Take perfect from perfect, the remainder is
perfect.'

Extract from *Eesha* Upanishad,
translation by W B Yeats.

# Glossary and Notes

This section augments and develops meanings given elsewhere in this volume and adds several further definitions. The terms listed give an insight into the philosophical background to Japanese poetry, and the Zen buddhist concepts which have tended to influence development of the *haiku*. The aesthetic ambience and special poetic terms relevant to haiku and senryn are fully explained in *Breathing with the Mind* (Element, 1993).

**Advaita:** non-dualism; teaches that *Brahman* and *Ātman* have the fundamental sameness of identity.

**Ahamkāra:** *aham* (I); *kāra* (Maker), sense of individuality and separation from others in the world.

**Ānanda:** 'bliss', synonymous with *Brahman*.

**Animism:** theory that both animate and inanimate objects are inhabited by spirits.

**Āryans:** Indo-European invaders of India during the second millennium BC. They eventually merged with the non-Āryan population.

**Ātman:** Universal self in the individual, identical with *Brahman* the all-pervading 'soul' of the Universe.

**Avidyā:** 'ignorance' – spiritual blindness preventing realization of the human being's oneness with *Brahman*.

**Bodhidharma:** traditionally, the Indian who first brought Ch'an (Zen) Buddhism to China.

**Bodhisattva:** an enlightened being who renounces entry into *Nirvāna* until all beings are saved.

**Brahmā:** God the Creator of the Universe.

**Brahman:** the Ultimate Reality, the Absolute of Hindu religion and philosophy – *nirguna brahman* (*without* qualities or conditions); *saguna brahman* (*with* qualities or conditions). The divine ground of existence – Absolute consciousness.

**Brahmin:** member of the priestly class of Hindus.

**Buddha:** *budh* (awake, understand). 'The enlightened one'.

**Buddhi:** the faculty of intellect and intuition.

**Caste:** the hereditary social system of India; division into groups which carry socio-religious values.

**Ch'an:** School of Chinese Buddhism (Zen in Japan) derived from 'Ch'an-na' a Chinese vocalization of the Sanskrit *dhyāna* (meditation).

**Chit:** Absolute consciousness; identical with *Brahman*.

**Chitta:** a level of the inner organ of mind (*antahkarana*), designated as substance of mind.

**Dhyāna:** contemplation; meditation.

**Duhkha:** unsatisfactoriness; the suffering resulting from a desire for permanence in the context of impermanance, that is, the world.

**Ekāgratā:** One-pointedness; single-minded attention.

**Gautama:** personal name of Buddha; his family name was Siddhārta.

**Gunas:** 'strands', three qualities or subtle elements of primary matter: *sattva* (harmony) *rajas* (activity) *tamas* (inertia).

**Guru:** teacher, spiritual guide.

**Hinayāna:** 'the lesser vehicle' the name accorded to the orthodox schools of early Buddhism by the adherents of the Mahāyāna.

**Ishwara:** *Īsh* (to rule) 'Lord' – a term used for God; 'Inner Ruler'.

**Jainism:** An Indian religion that rejects the authority of the Vedas. Jains do not believe in God but insist that divinity dwells in each soul. In Jainism, perfect souls are venerated as Supreme Spirit.

**Jīva:** 'living'; the individual soul of man.

**Jnāna:** from the root *jnā* (to know), knowledge or wisdom; knowledge of the ultimate reality, that is, the transcendent realization that Ātman and Brahman are one.

**Kāma:** love or desire – third of four Hindu aims in life.

**Karma:** action and the fruit of one's actions.

**Karuna:** compassion: the desire to relieve suffering in others; active sympathy.

**Kō-an:** Japanese form of the Chinese 'kung-an', meaning 'magistrates table' – a place where cases are tested in court. Paradoxical statement designed to baffle reason and confound logic.

**Lama:** this word has several meanings, ranging from 'spiritual master' to just a polite form of address for any Tibetan monk.

**Lingam:** phallic symbol closely associated with the God Shiva.

**Loka:** the world; the reality people create for themselves.

**Mahāyāna:** the 'great vehicle' – the form of Buddhism which spread to China, Japan and Tibet.

**Manas:** the lower function of the mind; discursive mind; attention.

**Mantra:** traditional formula which, when correctly repeated, is a powerful instrument for purifying, strengthening and enlightening the mind.

**Māyā:** the deluding projecting power of the Creator by which the universe has come into existence and appears to be real.

**Moksha:** liberation from the cycle of rebirths, *samsāra*; the ultimate goal of Hindu religion and philosophy.

**Mu-shin:** Japanese for 'no mind', meaning non-conceptualization. A seemingly negative attitude, it is the true ability to contact things directly and positively.

**Nāgārjuna:** the leading exponent of Mādhyamika, (a school of Mahāyāna Buddhism).

**Nirvāna:** 'blowing out'; enlightenment or liberation in which desires are extinguished.

**Pali:** the religious language of Theravāda Buddhism derived from a vernacular tongue of Northern India at around the time of Buddha.

**Prabhasvara:** brightly shining – used in relation to mind.

**Prakriti:** 'Making first or before'; primal substance; an eternal unconscious principle which is always changing. Composed of the three *gunas* called *sattva* (light) *rajas* (activity) and *tamas* (inertia).

**Pratyāhāra:** withdrawal of the mind from sense objects prior to the higher meditation.

**Pūjā:** worship in home or temple to any deity.

**Purusha:** Man, spirit within man, spirit. In Sāmkhya philosophy, one of two primordial categories – the other is *prakriti* (earth or matter). The intelligent principle; its essence is consciousness.

**Rāma:** *rām*, to rejoice. He who grants continuing joy.

**Reason:** the essence of true knowledge.

**Rig Veda:** oldest collection of Indian sacred texts.

**Rupa:** 'form'.

**Sacchidānanda:** composite term denoting *Brahman*, comprising *sat* (being), *cit* (consciousness) and *ānanda* (bliss) – the universal being.

**Sādhu:** Hindu ascetic.

**Samādhi:** concentration *sam* (with); *adhi* (Lord) – union with the Lord in which duality of subject and object disappear.

**Samskāra:** a residue or mental impression left by past experience; a latency or predisposition.

**Samsāra:** the continuous round of rebirths; the impermanence of the world.

**Sanskrit:** early language of the Indo-Āryans. The classical language of India; the name signifies 'perfectly constructed, cultivated literary speech.'

**Sat:** being; truth. That which is unbroken – term used for *Brahman*.

**Senryu:** this verse form is identical with that of the haiku. The founder of this poetic genre was Karai Hachiemon (1718–1790), whose literary name, Senryu ('River Willow'), was given to the derived form.

**Shakti:** divine power or energy, deified as a goddess.

**Shaman:** person, priest believed to derive special powers by means of direct connection with the supernatural.

**Shastras:** 'teachings'; textbooks of schools of Mahāyāna Buddhism.

**Shruti:** 'that which is heard': the sacred scriptures of Hinduism – especially the Vedas and Upanishads.

**Shūnyatā:** doctrine of 'emptiness' in Mahāyāna Buddhism.

**Smriti:** 'that which is remembered': writings of the Hindu religious tradition (less sacred than the *shruti*).

**Stūpa:** a shrine or mound associated with sacred places or relics of the Buddha.

**Sukha:** pleasure – that which is pleasing to the senses, mind and ego.

**Sūtra:** 'thread': aphorism or short verse summarizing basic teaching.

**Tantra:** 'loom': a group of medieval Hindu and Buddhist rites concerned with the divine energy (*shakti*) and sometimes orgiastic in character.

**Tao:** road, way – method: the unknowable. Principle above and within all that exists.

**Tathatā:** reality or 'suchness'.

**Theravāda:** 'The way of the elders' – the only extant form of Hinayāna Buddhism.

**Trimurti:** 'one God in three forms'; trinity of the gods Brahmā, Vishnu and Shiva.

**Turīya:** the Fourth (level of consciousness); union with Brahman. The other three levels are waking, dreaming and dreamless sleep.

**Upanishads:** final section of the Vedas or 'Vedānta'; embodying some of the earliest philosophical thought of India – particularly of the identical nature of *Brahman* and *Ātman*.

**Vairāgya:** desirelessness; non-attachment to objects.

**Virāt:** the physical universe as a manifestation of God.

**Viveka:** discrimination, discernment, reason. Ability to distinguish the Real from the Unreal.

**Yin-yang:** complementary opposing forces in nature expressed as male and female; light and dark; growth and decay, etc. Two principles of early dualistic philosophy.

**Yoga:** *yuj* – 'to unite'. Union, spiritual union. As a proper noun, alludes to the method of meditation and philosophy taught by Patanjali. The science of union of the individual soul with the Absolute.

**Yoni:** 'female sexual organ'; the base from which the phallic symbol of the *lingam* rises.

**Wu-wei:** 'without action'.

**Zen:** Japanese form of Ch'an – a school of Mahāyāna Buddhism. The written character '*zen*' means 'contemplation'.

**Zi:** (pronounced *tsu*) 'master'.